DANCING IN THE RAIN

JOHN LYONS

DANCING IN THE RAIN

A COLLECTION OF POEMS FOR CHILDREN

PEEPAL TREE

First published in Great Britain in 2015
Peepal Tree Press Ltd
17 King's Avenue
Leeds LS6 1QS
UK

ISBN 13: 9781845233013

Supported using public funding by
ARTS COUNCIL
ENGLAND

CONTENTS

Carnival Jumbie 9

Dancing in the Rain 11

Carnival Jumbie Dance Lesson 12

Carnival Moko Jumbie Dance 15

Setting a Trap for a Soucouyant 16

Fowl Play 17

My Dog Woopsin 19

Trini Manacou 20

Shadow Lost and Found 22

Looking for Duenne 23

Agouti Story 24

Betty's Breakfast 26

Our Cat Rasputin 27

Street-wise Pigeons 28

I Love Kentucky Fried Chicken 29

Iguana Chase 30

High Big Sky 32

Gold-eye Sarah 33

The Climbing Skeleton 35

Monica's Winter 36

Happy Snowman 37

Home Lover 38

Prankish Gnome 39

Crab Walk to Callaloo 40

Happy Hummingbird Food 42

The Visiting Bat 44

Z. Sprittle, Lepidopterist 46

Forbidden Fruit, Sometimes 48

Tell Me, Mama   50
Gru-Gru Beff   51
Plums for Hogs   53
Our Cook   55
Granny's Sugarcake   56
Natural Dancing Partners   58
Wakey! Wakey!   59
Mango-Head Joe   60
Monkey Say Cool Breeze   62
The Scared Crow   64
Pig's Boast   66
Solomon Big Gundy   69
Tadpole Comets   70
Happy Whales   71
School Dinner Swaps   72
De Time Ah Forget Me Lunch Box   74
Ah Bet You   75
The Hero in Daisy's Story   76
Carib Nightfall   78

For
Matilda, Felix, Betty, Remi.

CARNIVAL JUMBIE

Jumbie jump high
Jumbie jump low
Jumbie jumpin to calypso

Jumbie doin a dance
in de silk-cotton tree
he waitin for jouvay
an steelban music to breakaway

Jumbie jump high
Jumbie jump low
Jumbie jumpin to calypso

At six in de morning
steelban come out
people winin dey body
ole mas all about

Jumbie jump high
Jumbie jump low
Jumbie jumpin to calypso

Jumbie jump in a steelban
and everybody know
when he move he body
he's like black-smoke shadow

Jumbie jump high
Jumbie jump low
Jumbie jumpin to calypso

Jumbie have no flesh
he have no waist to hol'
buh jus look how he movin'
wid no bumsey to roll

Jumbie jump high
Jumbie jump low
Jumbie jumpin to calypso.

DANCING IN THE RAIN

And there we are again,
we go dancing in warm rain.

When sky set up with clouds
nearly charcoal black,
the yard cocks flap their wings
and let out a crowing, loud loud,
and the wind vex vex blowing strong,
baring hen fowls' feathered bums;
and everybody start grabbing
clothes off the clothes line;
we know rain coming.

Then we hear it getting nearer,
rattling on galvanize tin roof,
and as it drops down stinging hard,
squealing, we pull off we clothes;

and there we are again;
we love dancing in the rain.

CARNIVAL DANCE LESSON

One two three,
you can dance like me.

With arms held high
that's how you start,
let deh music touch your heart.

One two three,
you can dance like me.

Yuh muss be relax,
I insist, wine wid de riddum,
jerk yuh waist.

Shake up, jump up,
BACCHANAL!
Lehwe celebrate, is carnival.

One two three,
you can dance like me.

Jump in the band,
let us have some fun,
happy times have now begun.

One two three,
you can dance like me.

Boodum-di-dum!
Boodum-di-dum!

You can dance like me.

CARNIVAL MOKO JUMBIE DANCE

De carnival Moko Jumbie,
he so tall, tall, tall;
everytin' he see
over de people wall.

Moko Jumbie
on he long leg prancin-up;
dem people call it
de Moko Jumbie dance-up.

He prancin,
he dancin,
tossin talc and confetti.
Moko Jumbie
Moko Jumbie,
please don't dance on me.
Ah tellin yuh, ah only small.

SETTING A TRAP FOR SOUCOUYANT

One evening I saw my friend Ena Phillips
heaping a big set of rice on she front-door steps.

I shouted, "Ena, what you doing?
Rice is for cooking not for heaping!"

"Las' night," she said to me,
"a soucouyant suck me right here, above the knee,

and I did often hear my wise Granny say,
to keep a blood-sucking soucouyant away,

you must heap on your steps a lot of rice,
long grain, short grain, any kind would suffice;

and when soucouyant come to visit in the night
she must count each grain till morning light;

then 'crapaud smoke she pipe', boy, she done for;
she'll never fly and suck again, not anymore!

Trini sunlight with its fire and dazzle
sure to burn she up, fry she to a frazzle;

and this ugly, horrid, wicked thing
will no more pain and horror bring

to children sleeping in their beds
or fat cows munching in their sheds."

Well, with a rigmarole like that, what could I say,
I just "cheups" at Ena and went on my way.

FOWL PLAY

Midday come and de air
hot-heavy and still wid siesta quietness.

But not fuh long;
ah hear fowl cackling like mad
in de yard.

Ah find feathers plenty
all over de place.

When night come, ah see
empty places in de fowl-run.

Sly-sly mongoose,
he busy again.

MY DOG WOOPSIN

My mama, she love to joke;
she call meh dog Woopsin
after the calypso chorus:

"Woopsin, woopsin, la-ti-do…"

But Woopsin not funny at all,
he does bite before barkin first.
If yuh pass too close to 'im,
is SNAP, his teet in yuh ankle;
no use at all tryin to pull away,
Woopsin jaw lock hard an tight.

And as he look up at yuh
from the corner of he eye,
he seem to say, "Sorry, ah cahn
help it. Is de name she gimmeh
why ah so bad."

TRINI MANICOU

The marsupial Trini manicou
does not live like me or you.

At dead of night when we're fast asleep
this creature awakes and likes to creep

about to do a bit of scavenging,
sniffing out smelly, tasty things,

and it becomes so very fat,
it looks like a well-fed rat.

The manicou with its pouchy tum,
has another name: the opossum.

SHADOW LOST AND FOUND

Little Joe loved to see his shadow
following him wherever he went.

Then on a day when the sky
wore a dark, angry face,
Joe could not see his shadow.

He became very worried,
thought he had lost his shadow forever.

That night, he went reluctantly to bed,
closed his eyes tight as his mother said,
even counted up to a hundred sheep,
but he could not, could not fall asleep.

In the morning, he got out of bed
to see a happy sky smiling blue;

and where he stood he saw his shadow
long and slim securely attached to him
in its usual place along the ground,
his shadow lost, and then was found.

And everything was bright and right again.

LOOKING FOR DOUENNES

*(Douennes are prankish ghosts of children
in the bush and forest of Trinidad)*

Middle-ah-de-day
sun too hot for pitchin marbles.
Grandma takin she siesta in the house
shut-up to keep heat out.
Wid meh heart in meh mout,
ah went looking fuh Douennes

pass the big-big mango vert tree,
trou de shadowy cocoa grove,
cross de crayfish ravine
and into de bush, where
ah could hear soft chucklin:
Douennes at play fuh sure!

Ah tiptoe among dry bramble,
peek trou leaves. But all ah cud see
is two mountain doves dancing;
dey coo-cooin and prancing,
jus coo-cooin and prancing;
den dey begin to play piggy-back.
Buh wey de Douennes gorn?

AGOUTI STORY

Some Trinis hunt agouti for its meat;
they consider it a gastronomic treat;
but its tender flesh I don't want to eat.

Agoutis are wild and swift, can never be tamed.
They are nervous and shy; don't trust humans.
For this mistrust they should not be blamed.

This is why this story I am so eager to tell
you may find surprising. You must believe me!
This was no dream, it really did happen. Well,

while rambling in the forest on a sunny day
this adorable hare-like creature was standing
quite still in my path, about three strides away.

It lifted its head and began sniffing the air.
I stood transfixed, not moving a muscle.
Slowly it moved towards me standing there.

Nearer and nearer to me this agouti came.
I held my breath. My heart danced wildly.
Was it a dream, maybe a forest trick, a game?

It came so near, I could reach out, touch its head,
but wanting it to stay with me, not scamper away,
I pursed my lips, softly whistled a calypso instead.

A wonderful thing happened. It began to dance.
It was a strange animal, hind-legs prance;
believe me, it was a bizarre, magical circumstance.

And for about two minutes, maybe three,
we thoroughly enjoyed each other's company;
then a shock: this agouti vanished suddenly.

BETTY'S BREAKFAST

Betty's white pet hen, Florrie,
laid a brown egg for Betty's breakfast.

Thin soldier-toasts dip-spill
into runny, orange egg yolk.

"Muuum, where is the chicken
in Florrie's egg?

And Muuum, how did Florrie
get an egg inside her?

Why do chickens have drumsticks, Muuum;
and what does a chicken drum look like?"

OUR CAT RASPUTIN

Our grey tomcat Rasputin
has a peculiar but adorable grin,

not as broad as the Cheshire's,
but broad enough to give us pleasure.

Rasputin is a quick-witted cat
he grows fatter than our other cat, Jehosaphat,

who, though quite cute, is small and much thinner
because Rasputin steals his dinner.

STREET-WISE PIGEONS

You shouldn't be surprised
how street-wise city pigeons are,
the way they dodge among city buses,
play hide-an-seek with city cars.

And when they rest from their play,
they are still actively painting the city
a very messy white and grey.

Mind how you go,
don't slip.

I LOVE KENTUCKY FRIED CHICKEN

It's not impossible, and I tell you no lie,
I saw a whole Kentucky fried chicken
flying high up in the sky.

Its featherless skin was a golden brown.
I hailed it, shouting out its name,
but it continued flying, didn't come down.

It flew through clouds with the greatest of ease,
swooped and buzzed like ten trillion bees.

Then all of a sudden it disappeared
when it heard my mother's voice:

"Angie! Stop staring at that blank wall,
Eat up your spinach and mash
if you want to grow strong and tall."

IGUANA CHASE

Iguanaaaaaaaaaaaaaaaaaaaaaaaaaaaaaa!
Iguanaaaaaaaaaaaaaaaaaaaaaaaaaaaaaa!
The chorus cry through a Tobago village.

This iguana chase
is not really a dangerous race,
for this big lizard at large,
is talented with camouflage.

He darts for the nearest bush cover
and is instantly green all over.

When he remains stone-still on the ground
he is never easily found:
he changes to a groundish yellow.
As a reptile, he's a clever fellow.

HIGH BIG SKY

The sky is so big, far bigger than
my arms could ever spread wide.
Nowhere up there for a bird to hide.

The sky is so high, high, high
it goes up and up, never stops.

A man with a long grey beard,
with stars for eyes,
told me so in my sleep,
after I have been counting a hundred sheep.
So there, believe me or not.
See if I care.

GOLD-EYE SARAH

There's a bird in Tobago we call gold-eye Sarah;
beak and big eyes as yellow as hog plums.
She is a very early bird, this clever Sarah,
and always when foreday mornings come
she's already under the tree pecking sapodillas.

But sometimes, at night when I go to bed,
I keep my day clothes on to gain some time;
so in the mornings I am well ahead
of Sarah, still perched, waking-up in the lime
tree behind our rickety garden shed.

But I still love this brown, crazy-looking bird,
with roughed-up feathers and erratic hop.
She has an alarming cackle that's quite absurd,
like pebbles being thrown onto a tin roof-top.

THE CLIMBING SKELETON

I saw a human skeleton climbing a mango tree.
Its bones were rattling noisily.

From where I was standing
I could clearly see leaves caught
in the joint of its knee.

At such a sight,
Jumbie birds jumped out of their feathers,
caw-cawed wild songs,
scared bugs in secret shelters.

The rattling was strange music
with the wild cawing songs.
Blackbirds and sparrows,
rabbits out of their burrows
were all amazed to see
that rattling skeleton climb a tree.

MONICA'S WINTER

Sun, not here again today!
Please don't stay in the Caribbean
where Grandad comes from.

I begging you,
come over here to England
and drive the cold days away.

HAPPY SNOWMAN

The winter sun
is particularly bright today
with a constant array
of happy humour.

Look how by midday
it has completely
melted our snowman
into floods of happy tears.

HOME LOVER

I love my home underground;
no eyes for darkness in the earth.

Through my skin I feel where I am
and hear drumming up above.

When water seeps into my home
I feel the urge to move upwards.

Then there's a new feeling:
a dryness on my skin.
It is not like the earth's dark;

and I know nothing of bait hunters
or walking, running, killing boots.

PRANKISH GNOME

There's no space for football
on the front lawn I was always told.

Then one day our long-suffering,
weary, weathered gnome tripped me up.

I fell hard, went into darkness,
saw the gnome dancing happily among stars
to the music of our garden blackbird.

When my eyes blinked open from my doze
the gnome lay beside me with its painted stare,
a mocking, smile from ear to ear –
the white wound of its broken nose.

CRAB WALK TO CALLALOO

This is a strange, strange story I have to tell
about Tobago land crabs with a mangrove smell;

how on a damp, moon-lit night
they "walked", gave Scarborough town a fright

by appearing in mythic millions;
some believed they counted trillions.

Normally, Tobagonians are not scared of crabs,
but, in these numbers, they panicked, grabbed

their precious things, began to run away
to the forested hills above Scarborough Bay.

But from the crowd, a lone voice cried, *Enough's enough,*
we're bigger dan dem, now lehwe get tough.

They stopped running, did what that lone voice said,
dropped their belongings, made a stand instead.

They began to grab those crabs one by one,
filled lots of sacks; and when they were done

there were no more crabs scuttling about
and the hills echoed with a triumphant shout

of all voices sounding as one: *Hurray! Hurray!*
Now we go mek dem smelly blighters pay.

Lehwe cook dem in our favourite, peppery stew,
dat finger-lickin, scrumptious callaloo.

HAPPY HUMMINGBIRD FOOD

Hummingbird
hummingbird
humming a tune,
happy in June
(when flowers
and roses bloom)
sipping nectar
its favourite food,
loved also by bees.
They both enjoy it
with a natural ease.

THE VISITING BAT

Imagine my great surprise
to see a winged creature
like a mouse that flies.

Uninvited, it flew through a window
right into our room, where it flapped
around, nowhere further to go,

closely observed by Sylvie
our fat, hunter cat who rose
from the cushion where she sat.

She had the light of excitement
in her eyes, fixed on the flight
of a hearty meal just the right size.

My dad, agile with his old felt hat,
tried to capture that clever, dodging bat;
but they soon grew very tired

(and this is the bit that I most admired),
my dad flopped into an easy chair
and the bat landed "plop" into his hair,

where, resting, it was caught quite easily.
My dad reached up, and ever so gently,
cupped the tired bat in his hands.

He set it free into the dark, dark night,
saved it from a cat-eaten plight.
Sylvie was disappointed, of course.

She is fond of bats; in her experience,
she thought them tastier than rats.

Z. SPRITTLE, LEPIDOPTERIST

Ella was not afraid of Mr. Sprittle
even when her black Scottie, Tic,
flipped back his ears, tried to tuck
his little tail between his little legs
and the back of his neck bristled.

No one looked at Mr. Sprittle's head
as large as a Halloween pumpkin,
his eyes, pinched nose and mouth
grouped close together in his face.
No one stole a glance at the coarse,
black hair sticking out from under
the cuffs and collar of his black suit.

But everyone marvelled at the blur
of his hands snatching bugs in flight.
No one dared speak to him but Ella,
who wanted to talk about her
collection of butterflies and moths.
But Mr. Sprittle never uttered a word;

he squeezed his features even closer
together and hissed strangely
through his crooked, yellow teeth.

One day, at a safe distance, Ella
followed Mr. Sprittle home. She stood
on a bin, peered through his window.
She saw Mr. Sprittle hanging, like
a shabby, black suit, on a clothes hanger.

Nearby, was a bristling, hairy creature
with a large head and a long, sticky tongue
flicking butterflies and moths into its mouth.

FORBIDDEN FRUIT, SOMETIMES

1

In Trinidad, mangoes
in other people's gardens
taste sweeter, always.

When you stand in the road,
to pelt dong mango,
yuh have to go an pick dem up
from under de mango tree.

Buh dere's always a bad, bitin Rover
barkin in dem people garden.

2

At home wid meh sticky-mango-juice face,
meh grandma gimmeh ah good lickin
wid ah tamarind switch.

Ah hear the switch in meh grandma han
whistlin trou de air:

Tek dis, **"Switch!"**
An dis: **"Switch!"**
Yuh mus not go: **"Switch! Switch!"**
in dem people garden: **"Switch! Switch!"**
to tief dey mango: **"Switch! Switch! Switch!"**

Afterwards, wid she face serious-serious,
she put smelly iodine on meh bite-up leg.
It sting me more dan the tamarind switch.
Buh dat dohn change nuttin;
mangoes still taste sweet sweet
from dem other people garden.

TELL ME, MAMA

Tell me, Mama,
where does the sun come from
in the morning?

Where does it go to
when it reaches the edge of the field?

Teacher said the world is round and spinning.
I am standing on the world, how come I don't feel dizzy?
And if the world is spinning,
why don't the seas and oceans spill out into space?

And if the world is round, as teacher said,
how come some fields and roads
remain flat for miles and miles and miles?

When we go walking in the moonlight
why does the moon follow us wherever we go?

Please Mama, tell me.
I want to know.

GRU-GRU BEFF

Fruit from a palm tree
prickly-prickly palm tree

gru-gru beff
gru-gru beff

shiny smooth skin
cracks like an egg shell

gru-gru beff
gru-gru beff

a yellow pulp
that's sticky-sticky sticky

gru-gru beff
gru-gru beff

hold it well
it's slippy-slippy slippy

gru-gru beff
gru-gru beff

suck it to the nut
hairy nut, hairy nut

gru-gru beff
gru-gru beff

crack it with a big stone
find its kernel

gru-gru beff
gru-gru beff

kernel inside
is chewy-chewy chewy

gru-gru beff
gru-gru beff

oh how I love
this gru-gru beff

gru-gru beff
gru-gru beff.

PLUMS FOR HOGS

Tobago hog plums
are yellower and bigger
than chilliplums.
Hog plums fool you
with their sweet, sweet smell;
they taste sour, sour.

Only hogs enjoy hog plums.
Guess why!

OUR COOK

My dad is really the greatest cook;
you won't catch him using a recipe book.

He says love is his best ingredient,
even more precious than a pot of gold,
and it can never, ever be bought or sold.

Believe me, whatever he cooks I eat,
whether green veg, tripe, pig trotters or real meat.

His food does me so much good. Everybody
should have their own cooking dad like mine
and they would be very happy all the time.

GRANNY'S SUGARCAKE

Sugarcake!
Sugarcake!
Ah chile sweetie ting
a Trini granny could mek:

She grate de coconut,
put sugar in ah hot pot.
When it bubble-up like crazy
she stir in de coconut;
den she drop in some clove,
ah piece of cinnamon,
an few drops ah vanilla.

She screwin up she face,
keepin she yeye pon it.
She stirrin it,
she stirrin it
an she whole body shakin-up;
ah tellin yuh,
meh Granny got riddum.

Wen de sugarcake ready,
she spoon it out
on greaseproof paper,

an is den meh mout begin to water;
but de look meh Granny gimmeh
tell meh ah got to wait
fuh it to cool down good.

Sugarcake!
Sugarcake!
How ah love de sugarcake
meh Granny does mek.

NATURAL DANCING PARTNERS

The willow and the wind
are natural dancing partners;
look how the willow weeps
with the joy of movement,
skillfully rooted to the spot.

Their knowing to move as one
is in the willow's supple limbs,
bending forwards, backwards,
swaying to the wind's strength
leading it this way and that.

WAKEY! WAKEY!

Who needs alarm clocks!

Every night just before
I turn off the lights in my room
and leap into bed under the covers,
I close the curtains, leaving
open a teeny-weeny gap.

In summer and spring mornings
day comes with the sun like a waking
sharp shaft of yellow light
through that gap in the curtains;

but in autumn and winter mornings
it sidles softly in, whispering,
"Wakey-wakey, wakey-wakey,"
till I open my eyes.

MANGO-HEAD JOE

Mango-head Joe, he so greedy
it tek bags ah food fuh feed he.

Me and meh pal, nicknamed Rab,
find im picnikin one day
cocky as a big blue crab
on de beach in Maracas Bay.

Ah tellin yuh,
mango skin and seed
all round he in de sand;
he was nyamin-up mango calabash
one in each hand.

Yellow mango juice
was all over he face.
To tell yuh de trute
he was a disgrace.

But ah only jealous;
I too, love calabash mango.

MONKEY SAY COOL BREEZE

(A Trinidad saying: sooner or later
you are going to get your just desserts)

Wat yuh have in yuh mout?

Remember yesterday
when I had meh sugarcake
an ah let yuh have a bite.

Wat yuh have in yuh mout?

It smell like paradise plum.
Tomorrow ah bringin a whole heap a pewah
to school, an yuh go want some.

Wat yuh have in yuh mout?

Ah bet it taste nice.
Remember how ah protec yuh
from Ziggy de school bully!

Wat yuh have in yuh mout? Tell meh nah!

If yuh doh gimmeh a bite
ah goin to tell teacher ah see yuh
kissin Telma in de playground durin recess.

Please, please; wat yuh have in yuh mout?

Ah go give yuh six ah meh bess agate marbles
fuh jus one chinkee, chinkee bite.

OK DEN! Ah doh care.
Keep dat nasty ting
in yuh mout.
Remember, *Monkey say cool breeze.*

THE SCARED CROW

A sparrow and a crow
were perched in a willow
at the edge of a cornfield.

"Scarecrows,
they don't scare me,"
cawed the crow.

"That may be so,"
said the sparrow;
"but, look again.
This one wears
a ginger cat
disguised as a hat."

PIG'S BOAST

"MOOOOOOO,"
said a big-uddered cow
to a big, fat sow,

"I don't know how
you can grow so big on
troughs of mushy food.
Does it taste good?
Does it really taste good?"

"Oink oink," replied
the big fat sow, "you
will never know how,
not now, not ever,
because you are bovine,
dumb, and I am clever.

I must tell you,
that time and time again,
humans have marvelled at
the quickness of my brain.

I am a real star
born to go far.
I've been on telly;
and I am very proud
of my biggish belly."

SOLOMON BIG GUNDY

On a can't-see-your-hands dark Saturday night,
Basdeo, my best pal, armed with an old torchlight
went hunting for crabs in the stinky mangrove
beyond the coastline railway track near Barataria.

He came back with a full-face smile
and an enormous blue crab
with a pincer gundy as big as a monkey wrench.

He was shouting out,
"Solomon Big Gundy,
yuh good fuh de pot!"

Sunday morning
he was still smacking his lips,
and licking all eight finger tips;
he so happy, he began to sing:

"Solomon Big Gundy,
ah ketch yuh on Saturday,
cook yuh in a callaloo,
eat yuh on Sunday;
and dat's de end of you,
Solomon Big Gundy."

TADPOLE COMETS

Tadpoles huddled in a pond
afraid of the Caribbean night,
its intense darkness.

Candleflies moving about,
lighting up and going out,
lighting up and going out.

The tiniest tadpole shouted,
"What's that, what's that!"

"They're comets, silly,"
cried Billy, the largest tadpole.

HAPPY WHALES

In the deep, wide sea
whales swim and blow
spouts and splash about.

"We are having a whale of a time,"
they sing to the sea,
the clouds and the sky.

SCHOOL DINNER SWAPS

Annie, my best friend at school,
likes eating my fried dumplings and saltfish accra.

I like her chip butties with tomato ketchup.
Annie and I have very happy lunch-times.

Granny is very happy too.
She likes my big appetite
for fried dumplings and salt fish accra.

DE TIME AH FORGET MEH LUNCH BOX

Meh Grandma roll she eyes to de sky,
and arms akimbo, she say,
"Laard, Laard, look at de crosses yuh givin meh
in meh ole age wid dis pickney,
to bring meh heart failure."

Den she cut she vex-vex eyes at meh and bawl,
"Yuh better go an get dat lunch box
if yuh know wat's good fuh yuh!"

Trouble is, night comin dong fass
an de school two runnin-miles away,
close close to ah buryin groun.
Wat's more, dem people say
de school haunted. Dey hear
jumbie bird playin de school piano
makin ah whole heap ah noise
in de dead-a-night.

Ah had to climb trou de window.
Ah tellin yuh, ah had to do it,
ah had to do it.

When ah stop runnin, ah find mehself
back home in de kitchen
wid de lunch box.
Ah loss meh voice.
Couldn't say a ting to Grandma.
Buh she still not happy;
boy, if yuh see she face!

AH BET YOU

Yuh never seen
a moon so big big
as in the Caribbean.

Ah bet yuh,
yuh never eat a mango
hangin on de stem from a mango tree,

or beat-up a Bobolee
on Good Friday,
or suck a yellow and pink snowball
on Easter Sunday

after eatin a plate of rice and peas;
or pick pollen cheese
from de stamen of ah hibiscus flower
or jump-up in midday rain
as in ah warm, warm shower.

Ah bet you!

THE HERO IN DAISY'S STORY

Jack barged in
with a cheeky grin,
flexing his biceps,
disturbing Daisy's writing.

He insisted
on being the hero
in her adventure story;
refused to leave
until she agreed
to make him the hero.

But, he could not know
and she did not tell him;
she decided there and then
to give the hero
a very sticky end.

CARIB NIGHTFALL

In the Caribbean
at the end of day
sun drops suddenly
like a fire ball
behind forested hills,
and into the sea.

Steam clouds,
of red and orange,
shaped like monsters
float up into the sky
and for an instant
hover there.

Kisskadees
and sici-yea birds,
in awe of the sky
and the dark rushing in,
leave night music to
bull frogs' croaking bass,
high octave tunes
of mosquito violins,
and crickets' twitterings.

ABOUT THE AUTHOR

John Lyons was born in Trinidad. He came to the UK many years ago, and lives in Ely. He has established a reputation as a fine poet, a successful artist and an imaginative cook.

He has published five previous collections of poetry, *The Lure of the Cascadura*, *Behind the Carnival*, *Voices from the Silk Cotton Tree*, *No Apples in Eden* and *A Carib Being in Cymru*, and a cookery book, *Cook-up in a Trini Kitchen*. A contributor to numerous anthologies, John Lyons has read on radio, television and at many national and international festivals.

He is a Windrush Award Winner, Arts Achiever of the Year 2003. He was Co-Founder and Trustee of Hourglass Educational Arts Development Services (HEADS), 2000-2010.

ALSO BY JOHN LYONS

Cook-Up in a Trini Kitchen
ISBN: 9781845230821; pp. 256; pub. 2009; price: £19.99

Cook-Up in a Trini Kitchen not only contains over 150 mouth-watering, Caribbean-flavoured recipes, but also beautiful watercolour paintings, drawings, poems, stories and anecdotes recounting experiences with food and cooking by the author, painter and poet, John Lyons.

The culinary inspiration for this book comes from John Lyons's all-abiding love of food and cooking as an added fulfilment to his diversely creative life. The recipes reflect the cultural fusion of the many nationalities that have played a part in the history of his native Trinidad and Tobago. The dishes range from the homely, traditional fare of his mother and grandmother, through to new recipes which are the results of his experimentation. This is food that combines philosophy and flavour, making *Cook-up* a real feast of a book, not only for those who enjoy good food and cooking, but also for lovers of fine art, poetry and story-telling.

Contents include:
Snacks and Starters, Fish, Chicken, Meat, Soups, Vegetable Dishes, Rice, Pasta, Salads, Desserts, Drinks, Marinades, Sauces, Poetry, Watercolours, Poems, Anecdotes and much more!